Advance Reviews for
Salt & Pepper Cooking

July 29, 2015, Kirkus Review: "With these funny stories, an award-winning chef reflects on the formative roles of food, family, and friendship in his life.

"Former executive chef and owner of Portsmouth, New Hampshire's Blue Strawbery restaurant, Haller (*Vie de France*, 2002, etc.) grew up during the Depression, a poor kid in a Chicago suburb. His working-class extended family and Old World neighborhoods inspired a fascination with eclectic food combinations. Whether watching his Grandma Hazel dispatch a barnyard chicken by spinning it overhead "like David with his sling" or splashing "a little Benedictine Brandy on fried eggs after I heard Betty Grable order eggs benedict between dance numbers," it's clear that his insatiable curiosity about food began early. A young Italian girl, Louisa, became Haller's childhood friend and introduced him to cannoli, which easily eclipsed his grandmother's tapioca and butterscotch puddings. Growing up with many rural relatives, Haller paints a vivid picture of a bygone era with recollections of dinners fit for farmhands and the "womenfolk" preparing massive harvest feasts. His financially strapped, city-dwelling parents had more pedestrian palates, favoring "hot dog and beans…hamburgers, meat loaf, sloppy Joe's…creamed chip beef on toast…or my mother's tuna casserole." His mother's long hours waitressing required young Haller to prepare family meals, spurring a lifetime of culinary adventurousness, as he dished up string beans with pumpkin pie spices and lime and grape Kool-Aid baked into angel food cake for unwitting loved ones. Wit à la Ruth Reichl in *Tender at the Bone* (1998) invigorates these anecdotes throughout. Haller left for New York to make it as a writer and actor, often waiting tables to get by and eventually opening the Blue Strawbery in New Hampshire with some enterprising pals. Character sketches of family and friends here are as keenly observed and beautifully depicted as the food—the author's self-effacing humor a fantastic leavening agent.

"Flavorful serving of hilarious, poignant memories that will leave readers wanting seconds."

— *Kirkus Reviews*

"Chef Haller's inspiration and techniques have turned a small town in New Hampshire into a culinary destination. He is truly the Father of Cooking in Portsmouth, NH, it is an honor to know him as a chef, author, friend. . . . *Salt & Pepper Cooking* is such a good feeling book — it left me with an ear-to-ear comforting smile on my face. I loved reading about how so many of his memories of food are always a reminder of the day or person."

— Jethro Loichle, Executive Chef, Ristorante Massimo, Portsmouth, New Hampshire

"The most inspiring chef our region has ever seen has written a book so inspiring that it was impossible to put down until every last sentence was read. Chef Haller paved the way for all of us cooking here now, and it was an incredible pleasure reading tales of his life and inspiring moments throughout his years."

— Matt Louis, Executive Chef and Owner of MOXY, Portsmouth, New Hampshire

"These charming vignettes of a young boy who learns sitting in his grandmother's kitchen with eyes wide open, that food can equal love and that creativity in the kitchen knows no bounds. They tell the story of how James Haller, a great chef, found inspiration at a very young age. I read *Salt & Pepper Cooking* in a single sitting. You won't be able to put it down."

— Kathy Gunst, a James Beard award-winning food journalist, Resident Chef for NPR's *Here & Now*, and author of *Notes from a Maine Kitchen*.

"James Haller is a legend who should be regarded in the same breath as his better known contemporaries. In 1970, while California cuisine was just being born, Chef Haller was creating a courageous style of New England cuisine that had no peer in the American restaurant landscape. The menus of his fabled restaurant, Blue Strawbery, drew inspiration from what was on hand, but also from the rich heritage of Haller's childhood kitchens. This book gives readers a chance to peer into the mind of a developing cook, sharing the wide-eyed wonder that comes with the most creative minds. The details and dialogue in these anecdotes will make you wish you grew up alongside "Buddy," buoyed by family and friends as he navigated the difficulties and conquests of youth. He reminds us that, when times are tough, a love of food can keep us going. I am honored that my restaurant, Black Trumpet, lives the legacy of Blue Strawbery every day, and when I cook in the kitchen of 29 Ceres Street, I keep in the back of mind a pledge, that I will do my best to make Chef Haller proud."

—Evan Mallett, Executive Chef and Owner, Black Trumpet Bistro, Portsmouth, New Hampshire

"The storytelling is wonderful."
—Gregg Sessler, executive chef, Cava, Portsmouth, NH

"A revealing memoir of both Chef Haller's formative years and and evocative tableau of an American landscape though past, is still part of a continuum of both his life and ours. Full of the author's personal and infectious enthusiasm for food and cooking. Chef Haller deftly equalizes down-home and haute cuisines: from Mr. Bronstein's flattened (perfect) grilled cheese sandwiches to Chef Haller's own Cornish hens in sour cream, mushroom port sauce, the author refuses to play favorites among life's culinary bounty. *Salt & Pepper Cooking*, like Chef Haller's food, leaves the reader/diner wishing for more of that rich and flavorful goodness!"

— Matthew Sharlot, Chef / Owner, The Wellington Room, Portsmouth, New Hampshire

BOOKS BY JAMES HALLER

Cooking in the Shaker Spirit (with Jeffrey Paige)

The Blue Strawbery Cookbook, or Cooking
(Brilliantly) Without Recipes

Another Blue Strawbery, More Brilliant Cooking
Without Recipes

What to Eat When You Don't Feel Like Eating

Vie de France: Sharing Food, Friendship, and a
Kitchen in the Loire Valley
(*Soon to be republished with a new title:* A Little
Kitchen in France)

Simply Wonderful Food: A Cookbook for Men
with Prostate Cancer

Praise for *Vie de France*

to be republished in 2016 as

A Little Kitchen in France

"A charming narrative . . . Perhaps we can't reproduce these dishes exactly, but anyone with a feel for food can undoubtedly come close. As the few remaining days in Savonnieres tick away, we're left to wish that the clock would stop . . ."

— *The Union Leader*, Manchester, NH

"James Haller makes the reader feel like a welcomed, coddled, and well-fed seventh guest during his dream-come-true stay at Savonnieres in the heart of the Loire Valley."

— Susan Simon, author of *The Nantucket Table*

". . . a beguiling tale of a month in France when the living was easy, the friendships warm, and the food superb. An elegant tribute to friendship and joie de vivre that France still offers. Refreshingly, Haller is as much intent on celebrating friendship as the good life abroad."

— *Kirkus Reviews*

"The key to this uplifing biographical month is how important friendship is to the human condition . . . an inspirational toast to the stimulation of camaraderie that is a human need in order to live precious life to the fullest."

—*BookBrowser*

JAMES HALLER

Salt *And* Pepper Cooking

෴

The Education of an
AMERICAN CHEF

JAMES HALLER

Salt *And* Pepper Cooking

∽

The Education of an
AMERICAN CHEF

John Byrne, editor

Great Life Press
Rye, New Hampshire
2015

ISBN: 978-1-938394-17-1

Library of Congress Control Number: 2015949003

published for the author by

Great Life Press
Rye, New Hampshire 03870
greatlifepress.com

cover design and layout by Grace Peirce

Publisher's Cataloging-in-Publication Data

Haller, James, author.
    Salt & pepper cooking : the education of an American chef / by James Haller ; John Byrne, editor.
    pages cm
    ISBN 978-1-938394-17-1
    ISBN 978-1-938394-18-8
    1. Haller, James. 2. Cooks--United States--Biography. 3. Autobiographies.   I. Title.   II. Title: Salt and pepper cooking.

    TX649.H3445A3 2015   641.5092
                                            2015949003

I dedicate this book with love, respect, and gratitude to

Stephanie Voss Nugent

Who had the insight to recognize the value in these essays
And the courage to put them on the stage for

ACT ONE
at the West End Studio Theater
in Portsmouth, New Hampshire
Thank you, Stephanie

Contents

Preface

When I was a baby my mother worked as a waitress in Mrs. Hinemann's Tearoom in Oak Park, Illinois. As a single mother she had little money for day care, but Mrs. Hinemann was good enough to allow her to bring me along to work with her. I was put into a high chair in the kitchen where the cook could keep an eye on me. I'm told he would give me food to play with: carrots, mashed potatoes, pieces of bread. Food has been a toy ever since.

I simply love to cook. Whatever else is happening in my life, anger, disappointment, even sorrow, when I go into the kitchen that love of cooking is always there. I start with an idea of what I want the taste to be and then work backward until I have the first step. Sometimes the outcome is very different from what I expected, which to me is the cooking loving me back.

It isn't important to me if I don't replicate the same taste every time. I might say, "I wonder what will happen if I add this?" and so I add it. And I might use whatever that wonderful ingredient is in that composition again but then I will change something else. I never want the taste to be the same twice.

Because I always worked with what was fresh in the market, or what local farmers brought in to me, I found it difficult to make a menu even days in advance. I was never certain what would be in season and, more importantly, what would be inspiring. I would often make changes the day I cooked. What matters to me is, how does it taste?

Food is beautiful. Cooking is beautiful, the movement of my arms as they stir and grate and whip is like a dance, the romance of the scent of an herb roasting on a mound of sizzling pork, the feel of fresh dough engulfing your hands as you knead, the poetry of mixing combinations: lavender in a chocolate flan, smoked mussels in a cream soup touched with sherry, or breast of pheasant butterflied in apricot brandy and sour cream.

There is a beauty in the way food brings people together. To spend an afternoon in the company of friends and families, sharing platters of thinly sliced prosciutto and salamis, soft cheeses that came from a sheep or a goat or a bison in a distant land, fresh herbs over ripe tomatoes, for a taste that makes you feel that you are on the edge of a forest just after a rain, and bread that has a crust so light it barely crunches against your teeth on that first bite.

The lessons that came to me informally in the daily cooking of the households and kitchens of which I was a part, have stayed with me all my life. It is these informal venues that I bring for your entertainment.

Acknowledgments

I would like to thank John Byrne for his editing, Stephanie Voss Nugent for her critical support, Kathleen Soldati for opening the door on this new time in my life, Chef Patrice Gerard for inviting me into his kitchen, Dan Densch for his professional guidance, Adam Hosack for his brilliant tutoring, Grace Peirce for her work in helping to publish this material, the inspiration gleaned from the Monday Memoir Mob, to all of the men and women who have and will ever cook in Portsmouth, New Hampshire, and continue to make it the restaurant capital of New England, and lastly Abie Berggren at South Side Fitness in Dover, New Hampshire, for keeping me in remarkable condition so I can continue cooking, writing, and being happily healthy.

Chocolate

⟡

When I was three years old, I was placed for a
time in a state-supported foster home owing
to family and financial difficulties. The foster home
was an old farmhouse in Downers Grove, Illinois,
owned by Mr. And Mrs. Winter. Mealtimes were
communal, and visits were treated as social occasions
for the entire household.

I vividly remember being visited there by my
mother. On this day she had brought me a nickel-
sized Hershey bar, a sumptuous extravagance in those
waning days of the Great Depression. We sat in the
front parlor with Mr. and Mrs. Winter and the other
five foster children then boarding there.

"Now, Buddy," Mrs. Winter admonished, "don't
you think it would be nice if all the children had a
taste? You don't want to be known as selfish, do you?"

My heart fell, but obediently I unwrapped the
Hershey bar and broke it into several small pieces.

Using the top of a Tinker Toy can as a tray, I sullenly passed from child to child, as Mrs. Winter had instructed me, until only the very smallest piece was left for myself.

I held the velvety taste of that morsel in my mouth until it had dissolved and finally was gone. This fragment of sweetness that my mother had given to me I hadn't wanted to share or even eat. I had wanted to keep it for myself, like a part of her that wouldn't be leaving on the next train.

If, as psychology has taught us, we go through life seeking compensation for what was lost to us in our childhoods, then my life long passion for chocolate must be rooted in this early experience: the Hershey bar that I had been forced to share at Downer's Grove and my own small portion, that had melted away leaving an unfulfilled desire for more, like the anguish that assailed me at the thought of my mother's impending departure on a train that I was unable to stop.

Chocolate had become for me the symbol of love and self-worth, and like the chocolate, I never seemed to get enough of either.

The Grilled American Cheese Sandwich

⁓

A few months later we moved into a one-bedroom flat in Forest Park, Illinois, a flight up from a drugstore owned by Mr. and Mrs. Bronstein. Childless, the Bronstein's spent their time from early morning till late in the evening working at the store.

Mr. Bronstein was the pharmacist. He filled the prescriptions, did the ordering, and made sandwiches, while Mrs. Bronstein waited on the customers, made sodas, set up the displays, and kept the store immaculate. Apparently they had fallen completely in love with me, and I was permitted to visit with them whenever I chose.

One afternoon, while my mother was at work and my father was busy putting together one of his model airplanes, I wandered downstairs for a visit.

That day Mr. Bronstein taught me to make a

grilled cheese sandwich. Buttering two slices of white bread, he put two slices of dark yellow American cheese between the un-buttered sides and laid it on the flat-grill where he toasted it to a golden brown. Turning it over to toast the other side, he set a dish on top of the sandwich.

"Don't forget," I can remember him saying, "y' got to put a little plate on the top to make it flat and easy to eat."

As far as I'm concerned, Mr. Bronstein's grilled cheese sets the standard for that sandwich. He'd serve it to me with a fancy cut pickle on the side and one of Mrs. Bronstein's chocolate malteds: two huge scoops of vanilla ice cream, four squirts of chocolate syrup, four heaping spoons of Horlick's malt, and a pint bottle of milk. The little green and silver machine buzzzzed and whirrrred, whipping the mixture into a velvety smooth consistency that she poured into a tall glass, adding a giant dollop of whipped cream, and served it placed on a dish with a paper doily, a little glassine bag of two cookies, and two straws. There was always at least enough of that elixir left to refill my glass a second time. I remember telling Mrs. Bronstein she made the best malteds I ever tasted, and she told me it was because "I put a little extra chocolate and malted in. That's how you make things taste good. Always add a little extra."

After I'd eaten she would wash my hands and

face and comb my hair half a dozen times. And then she would let me smell all the colognes. Mr. Bronstein would carry me around on his shoulders and tell me stories until it was time for me to go home.

On the day that my mother announced to the Bronsteins that we were moving, as an economy, into a rooming house several blocks away where we would share the kitchen and bathroom with the other roomers, they were broken-hearted. So enamored of me, they even offered to adopt me. My mother declined and, after we moved, I never saw the Bronsteins again.

Though I have no clear memory of their faces, I do remember their love and kindness toward me, and the green marble counter top at the fountain, and what it felt like being lifted onto the dark green leatherette stool with the chrome trim.

Whenever I'm in need of a little reassurance, I butter two slices of plain white bread, put two slices of dark yellow American cheese in the center, lay the first buttered side into a low-flamed frying pan and, when it has toasted to a golden brown, I turn it over to the other buttered side, never forgetting to place a little plate on top so I will have a nice flat grilled cheese sandwich that's easy to eat, just like Mr. Bronstein taught me.

Egg Plant and
Angel Food Cake

The summer after we had moved into the rooming house we took the Dixie Flyer out of Chicago's Union Station to visit my father Jimmy's mother Hazel and his stepfather Emory, in Sullivan, Indiana. Emory came to meet us at the station and drove us back to their little farm.

The first time I ever saw my Grandma Hazel she was killing chickens for dinner. I was four years old at the time and thought it was about the most interesting thing I had ever seen. Cornering a generous-sized hen, Grandma Hazel seized her up with a predatory swoop, and mid its squawking, scoped out a second victim. After this hen had been snatched up, she grabbed the first by its head, swinging the body in a circle above her, like David with his sling, until it flew, disconnected from the neck.

"That's one!" she yelled, tossing the severed head into a corner of the yard, and then repeated the show with the remaining victim. "That's two!"

"They're still alive!" I shouted in delighted amazement as the disconnected bodies jerked about the chicken yard, blood and dirt smearing the white feathers.

"Aw no they ain't," Grandma Hazel laughed, "It's just some old nerves. C'mon and we'll gut 'em."

Unable to cope, my mother retired, traumatized, to the porch swing at the other side of the house, but I followed Grandma Hazel eagerly, fascinated. There, at the tender age of four, I learned how to stalk, kill, gut, and then soak a chicken in hot water to make the feathers easier to pluck, and finally, how to cut the bird into pieces and cook them.

Dipped in beaten egg, then rolled in breadcrumbs and fried in a pan with about a quarter inch of sizzling lard, these pieces would be salt-and-peppered, fried crisp on all sides, then covered and turned down low to cook until a crusty golden brown on the outside, tender and juicy on the inside.

Mashed potatoes with a thick and creamy milk gravy were always served and either corn on the cob, or green beans fresh out of the garden cooked with a rasher of bacon. There was a salad of lettuce, tomatoes, and rosette radishes, homemade baking powder biscuits with butter and strawberry preserves, and for dessert a cherry or gooseberry pie and every bit of it, except the flour, came from their own little farm.

Emory was a foreman for the state department of roads. He and Hazel got up in the middle of the night and by four Emory was fed and out of the house. By the time we got up grandma Hazel had already picked and pitted cherries off the tree for a pie and prepared an enormous breakfast for us of fresh eggs, country ham with hominy grits, and piles of toast from home-made bread with jam.

The noonday meal was always the largest, when the heaviest food was served in the greatest quantity. Supper, on the other hand, was often sliced cold meat left over from dinner, a salad, and fried eggplant.

Grandma Hazel peeled her eggplant and sliced it into half inch thick pieces, which she salted and let sit overnight to leach out the excess water, leaving the vegetable more firm for frying. Before cooking it, she would rinse, then blot it off, dip it in egg and cracker crumbs—she was very particular that they be cracker crumbs—and fry it in shortening to a toasty brown on both sides. Salt and pepper were the only seasonings she ever used. The taste was unmistakably eggplant. No herbs, no spice, not even garlic. Pure eggplant and we ate mounds of it.

On Sunday mornings she baked the Commu-nion bread for the little Christian church to which they belonged and where Emory was a deacon. The

Communion bread was a large, crisp, thin, almost cracker sort of bread, perfectly round and about eighteen inches in diameter. There were always two, wrapped in a white linen cloth and carried on silver trays. The bread was passed from member to member with a tray of tiny glasses of grape juice. When I got older, I was invited to partake.

Now, as a child completely immersed in pre-Vatican II Catholic culture, I knew it was a mortal sin for me to sit in on other religious services and even more damning to receive their Communion, but, I thought since I was in Indiana, maybe God couldn't see me.

The highlight of any occasion was Grandma Hazel's angel food cake. Beating thirteen egg whites into a meringue using just a fork, she made the tallest angel food cakes I've ever seen, elegantly decorated with a "seven minute" icing that never failed.

Grandma Hazel swirled that seven-minute icing lavishly over that tall, heavenly cake using only a table knife and decorated it with plump, out of the garden strawberries. It surely was the most wonderful angel food cake ever, served by a woman who found great joy in her culinary ability to evoke a smile of awed satisfaction from the small out-of-towner sitting at her table.

Every now and again I'll taste a piece of cake that reminds me of hers, and for an instant I see that wide green field next to Grandma Hazel's little white farmhouse and the line of trees along the dusty road that ended at the back porch of her kitchen door. And just for a moment, that instant, it's all still there, and me with it.

Milk Soup and Kluskis

∽

For a time we lived with my maternal grandmother and her husband, my grandpa Bill.

Cooking came naturally to Grandma Agnesia and her sisters: Celia, Estelle, Eulalia, Lucille, Sophie, and Polly, the Kostecki girls. They seldom resorted to recipes yet never appeared at a loss or ill at ease. In retrospect I can see they must have imparted this confidence to me.

When I was two years old I woke early one morning before my grandparents, went out to the kitchen, and mixed together a bag of flour, a quart of milk and a dozen eggs . . . with their shells. I was making pancakes.

Grandma often related this story.

"You should have seen the mess. But what got me," she would say, with evident satisfaction, "was that he had all the ingredients right."

We spent many happy hours in her kitchen

15

together. When I was five years old, she taught me to make *kluskis*, a simple noodle made with a couple of tablespoons of flour and an egg, mixed in a coffee cup to the consistency of a thick molasses, then slowly dropped into an eddy she had stirred into a boiling broth.

Sometimes she would make these noodles in a milk soup that she seasoned with salt, pepper, and a huge lump of butter. When my uncles went out for a night of carousing, she would feed them this soup, which she believed coated their stomachs to ameliorate the effects of too much alcohol.

Cooking with my grandmother is one of the happiest memories of my childhood. She was a model of cooking liberated from the restraints of recipes. I never saw her measure, or look on a page of a cookbook to follow any prescribed culinary agenda. She always knew how much flour, how much milk, or how much butter was needed and the food she was cooking always came out perfectly, from roast veal with creamed kohlrabi to her devil's food cake with black walnuts and coffee icing.

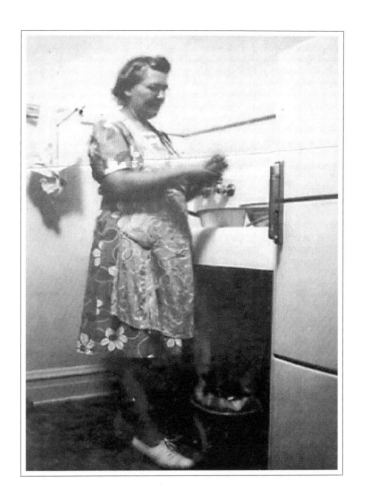

KENTLAND CAFE — KENTLAND, INDIANA

The Kentland Cafe

ぐて

After Grampa Bill retired, he began letting us take his 1937 DeSoto on these trips to Grandma Hazel's.

My mother would start packing suitcases weeks in advance for our yearly visits to Sullivan. On the morning of our departure, my brother and I were dragged out of bed at my father's insistence, at five in the morning to "get an early start." By six we were on the road. A trip of a little more than three hundred miles, but in those pre-interstate days, in the ten-year-old DeSoto, it took about seven hours.

Once on the road, Milly would begin a running critique of Jimmy's driving.

"Watch how you're driving now. You don't have to pass everything on the road."

My father looked straight ahead, his blue eyes faded to the color of hard steel. "Don't worry about it, will you?" he muttered, digging in his heels.

"Don't worry about it? If I don't worry about it who will?"

"You want to drive?" he asked her.

"I just want to get there in one piece, that's all," she answered, opening the side vent to let in some air.

The miles passed in uneasy silence. In the back seat my little brother Jerry and I read comic books or played "I spy" to escape the tension. When I became bored, I would begin to tease Jerry. If my provocations became blatant enough to threaten the peace, my father would make eye contact, staring back at me out of the reflection of the rear view mirror. Other than this, his attention remained focused on the road ahead.

"Look at that speed! My God, slow down . . . you want to get us all killed?" my mother asked.

"I'm only going forty-five," he protested.

"Forty-five?" she retorted. "Like hell you were. You were doing almost sixty!"

"I was not." He answered, gripping the wheel.

"Don't tell me," she countered, (as though anyone could), "you were too."

"You can't tell from the passenger seat," he insisted dismissively. "It looks higher because you're looking at it on a slant."

In response, my mother leaned over the stick shift practically onto his lap and stared pointedly into the speedometer.

"Oh yeah? Well I'm looking at it right now and I'm telling you it's the same way I was looking at it before and you were going over fifty-five!"

At this my father lifted his foot from the pedal, allowing the car to decelerate until finally we were crawling along at maybe fifteen or twenty miles an hour.

"Oh sure. Now you're gonna be smart," my mother said, but still he did not accelerate and we continued at this snails pace a few miles further before she finally exploded.

"All right! That's enough now! Are you deliberately trying to drive me crazy?" she asked rhetorically. "Because if you are, you're succeeding!"

The three of us knew this line by heart.

"Jimmy, if you don't speed up this car, I'm going to open the door and jump out," she announced dramatically. "Right here, honest to God, I'm warning you!" she said, clutching the door handle. Only then did he finally concede, stepping on the gas in the hope, perhaps, that if she really did jump he would be going fast enough to kill her.

I could see my mother's point though. The one week we had for a vacation and we didn't stop anywhere, not a state park or a wild life preserve or any point of interest, nothing. Occasionally we would pass roadside stands that sold jars of jelly, jugs of raspberry cider, and in those days, those chenille peacock bedspreads in rainbow colors that my mother admired so much.

"Look at those spreads," she sighed. "They're just beautiful. " 'Course," she added ruefully. "I'll never be able to afford one."

The trip was, simply, our house to Grandma Hazel's and Grandma Hazel's to home, with only one stop in between at the half-way-point, Kentland, Indiana, where we always ate our lunch at the Kentland Cafe.

The proverbial "wide spot in the road," Kentland's Main Street was old U.S. 41. As I recall there was a hardware store and a feed store, a furniture store, a dry-goods, and up the road about a block out of town, another restaurant. Which we never stopped at.

"Too remote," my father said.

"Uh oh," my mother would begin sarcastically, feigning surprise as we turned into the parking lot. "We must be half way and, oh look, what a surprise!" she continued with mock delight. "The Kentland Cafe! Aren't you surprised, Buddy? How about you, Jerry?"

But we knew enough not to answer, understanding that it would be wiser to say nothing than risk antagonizing one parent by agreeing with the other.

Inside the cafe, we settled into one of the red Naugahyde booths by the windows overlooking the highway. The waitress arrived with glasses of water and the menus, which Jimmy perused with the same focus previously applied to the road.

Though, as far as I can recollect, the Kentland Cafe's menu was as unvarying from year to year as the flat open farmland through which we had been driving all morning.

"It's the same menu every year," my mother carped in exasperation. "What the hell do farmers know about eating?" she asked, looking heavenward.

My mother, whose family all lived in Chicago, liked to contrast her citified attitude to the small town mentality of her in-laws, dismissing them as a bunch of farmers.

But in fact, though he had grown up in a tiny mid-western town, Jimmy had never been a farmer. In actuality, it was my mother who'd been born to farmers, raised in the little Polish farming community of Pulaski, Wisconsin until she was ten.

After we had placed our order, my mother, who worked most of her life as a waitress, began scrutinizing the edges of the water glasses for leftover lipstick smears, and moistening her napkin in her own glass, to add finishing touches to the table top. I always felt that it was my mother, not the waitress, who should have gotten the tip.

Tacked above the pass-through window into the kitchen was an oversized postcard of a busty woman in front of a woodland pond being ogled by a bear

hiding behind a tree, the seat of her pants sugges-
tively ripped on a berrybush. The caption read: "SHE
JUMPED IN HERE WHEN SHE SAW THE BEAR
BEHIND."

People who read it shook their heads and
chuckled an amused "ain't that somthin'."

But not my mother.

"How come it's always a woman?" She wanted
to know. "Sure, you never see some man with *his* tail
hangin' out. It's always a woman being made fun of."

Jimmy shook his head and snickered, "You're just
overly sensitive, That's your problem."

"You're damn right that's my problem," she
slammed back.

When the food arrived, Milly immediately
opened Jerry's sandwich to be certain there was nothing
but the bread and cheese. If so much as a stray pickle
slice had been left as a garnish on his plate he would
begin screaming until it had been removed. Next she
would re-arrange her own sandwich, picking off tiny
bits of wilted lettuce, scraping off excess mayonnaise
and replacing the tomatoes on top of the bacon. The
ice in her iced tea, which was hot tea poured over ice,
had by this time melted into four tiny cubes.

"Uh, Miss? You think I might have a little ice for
the iced tea?" she asked. And then, as an aside to the
three of us, "Y' think they'd just make a pitcher of tea
and put it into the refrigerator and then they'd have it?

Boy, I tell you, that's what I mean about a small town mentality."

On one of these annual visits, I remember the screen door opening and a woman of about sixty appeared in a blue checkered housedress, with pin curls in her gray hair. Stepping up to the pay phone at the entrance, she dropped a nickel into the slot, and rang up the operator.

"Vi? Gimme Martha, will ya? Uh huh, two long and a short, ring three." There was a slight pause while the transaction took place.

"Martha? Martha, it's me." Leaning into the mouthpiece she shouted. "ME, EDNA." After another slight pause she answered "FINE! I SAY I'M FINE."

At this the cook stuck his head through the pass-through to see what the commotion was all about.

"WE TOOK DAD IN THIS MORNIN' FOR ONE A THEM EKG THINGS!" she continued. "I DUNNO . . . CARDIO . . . TEST YOUR HEART, I GUESS. I SAY, TEST YOUR HEART."

"WELL, HE'S OKAY. DOC SHELBY SAYS HE'S JUST OLD . . . OLD! . . . WELL I GUESS HE SHOULD KNOW. . . . HE'S THE SAME AGE AS DAD!"

Glancing up at the clock, she concluded, shouting, "GOTTA GO MARTHA. JUST WANTED T'LET Y'KNOW . . . ALL RIGHT . . . ALL RIGHT . . . SURELY WILL, HON . . . BYE BYE."

Hanging up the phone, Edna smiled at the rest of us who had stopped midway in our lunch to listen, letting the screen door slam shut on her way out.

"She should've just gone to out to the porch and yelled," the waitress quipped. "Could've saved herself a nickel!"

Despite all her dissatisfactions, when it came time to pay the bill, my mother left a little extra in the tip.

Moistening the paper napkin in her water glass, she wiped my brother's face, instructing us, "If you've got to go to the toilet you better do it now. You know he's not going to stop till we get to Sullivan, and this'll be your last chance to use an inside toilet for a whole week. Boy, I tell you, farmers."

Kuchen

＜ツ）

Great-Aunt Estelle, my Grandma's elder sister, and her husband Pete, owned a Wisconsin dairy farm on the shores of Lake Michigan in a town called Port Washington, about thirty miles north of Milwaukee. "Port," as the family referred to it, was a three-hour drive from Chicago in the late thirties and early forties, and I often accompanied my grandmother and Grandpa Bill, to the frequent gatherings my mother's side of the family held there.

Great-Uncle Pete's house was built of fieldstone in an eastern European style, covered with a stucco cement that had aged over the years into a deep cream color. Just inside the back door was the long, spacious kitchen, with an oil-cookstove and the crank-up telephone just left of the doorway into the front hall.

Like the crank-up telephone, the pump in the kitchen sink, or the outhouse, the farm had many holdovers from the middle of the nineteenth century when it was built. Upstairs, all the mattresses were piszhinas (Polish feather beds), each one covered with a handmade quilt. The doors had latches, rather than the knobs to which I was accustomed, and each time I lifted them it was with a sensation that I was entering into a room from out of the past.

Both my grandmother and her sister Estelle had been married before. Their first marriages were typical of the Great Depression era, in which so many husbands, disconnected by their inability to support their families, simply abandoned their wives and children.

My grandmother's second marriage might have been considered happier than her sister's since my "Grandpa" Bill was a good-natured, kindhearted man as well as an able provider, whereas Uncle Pete, an old country Luxemburger, was dictatorial and often ill-tempered. But Estelle was up to his strong and sometimes overbearing personality and, in addition to running the house competently, she saw to directing much of the labor and the farm's accounts as well. Their marriage had made Estelle, with her two young children, a secure woman.

The children from her first marriage, Evelyn and Charles, continued living at the farm even after they had grown. Evelyn eventually married her step-brother Herb, Uncle Pete's son by his first marriage, and they became the parents of my cousins, Peter, Charlie, and Mary Delores. And so, though there were no direct offspring of Estelle and Pete's mid-life marriage, remarkably, they shared grandchildren in common.

Farming then was still a communal enterprise, and at baling or threshing time, the men would gather with their machinery, wagons, and tractors at each farm in turn, to bring in the hay crop for feeding their herds through the long winter.

In this season the "womenfolk" (as they used to be called) were expected to feed the crew a big noon-time dinner. No prizes were awarded but these all-out feeds were definitely a contest between kitchens. I would happily join my grandmother when she would visit up at the farm during such times to help Estelle and Evelyn with the cooking.

Uncle Pete and Herb would be up before it was light to milk their herd of Holsteins, Jerseys, and Guernsey, each taking a mason jar full of coffee out to the barn with them. At sunrise, the neighbor men began to arrive, and Aunt Estelle would bring them coffee out in the yard as they discussed the day's labor. By six o'clock they would be off to the fields, my cousins in tow.

But I always hurried back to the business of the kitchen. The smell of cooking and the women's laughing and joking as they worked made me feel that life was firmly planted, and that this basic effort that sustained it, cooking, was a wonderful time.

The breads would have been mixed and set to rise the night before, and as many as a half dozen freshly killed chickens, gutted and plucked for frying, would already have been in the pan. I recall the interest with which I would watch Aunt Estelle make what she called *kuchen*.

Kuchen is a Germanic word for cake. Uncle Pete and his first wife, who emigrated from Luxemburg with him, used to bake this cake, and when she died and Pete re-married, Aunt Estelle learned to make the kuchen as well. I watched her prepare it so many times that each step is committed to memory.

First scald a cup of fresh milk; let it cool for about ten minutes; then pour it over three cakes (tablespoons) of yeast, stirring until the mixture is well blended. Mix in a cup of flour and set the bowl in a warm place until it doubles in size.

Whip together a cup of sugar with a cup of butter until smooth and add five eggs, one at a time. Combining the risen yeast-flour-mix into the eggs, butter, and sugar, add three more cups of flour, a couple of hands full of seedless raisins, some walnuts, and the zest from an orange. Transfer the batter into a buttered tube pan, and let it rise again until it has doubled for the second time. Then bake it in a pre-heated oven at 350° F for about forty-five minutes.

When the kuchen had cooled, Aunt Estelle would dribble the top with a powdered sugar icing made with a couple of tablespoons of orange juice, a little butter, and enough powdered sugar to make it into a thin icing. I loved this cake. Light and airy, almost the consistency of bread, it was actually a tall coffeecake.

At noontime the men returned, washed off the chaff in the barn and waited outside for Aunt Estelle to push open the screen door and call "come and get it!" before tramping in. The round dining table had been opened up with the extra leaves, and there was already bread and butter sitting on it. Coffee was immediately offered, with sugar, and cream siphoned from the top of fresh milk.

There might be a baked ham rubbed with a mix of brown sugar and mustard and studded with cloves. Huge platters of chicken that had been shaken in flour and fried in lard, piles of mashed potatoes served with a cream gravy that had been made by sprinkling flour into the chicken drippings and then slowly stirring in milk until it begins to thicken. I remember vegetable dishes like mixed kale and cabbage that had been cooked in bacon, or sweet and sour beets done Polish-style with caraway seeds, white vinegar, and sugar. The hungry laborers heaped this wonderful food onto their plates, drenching mountains of mashed potatoes in the cream gravy.

For dessert, there was a plum pie and a peach pie with whipped cream, and of course, the kuchen that always was eaten to the last crumb. On the rare occasion when there was any left over, we'd cut it into slices and make French toast, which we ate sweetened with butter and sugar.

"Say, Estelle," I remember one of the farmers telling my aunt, "any time you get tired of this old fart (Uncle Pete), you can come over and cook at my house."

"Oh sure," my aunt returned, "and what about your wife?"

"Fine by me," Uncle Pete cut in. "Send your Missus my way. She's younger than mine anyway, she'll last longer."

After the men had returned to the fields, I helped clear away their plates and sat picking at the leftovers, listening to the gossip about the families of the men who had just been fed, while we waited for the dish water to get hot on the oil stove.

The big story in the summer of thirty-nine was Minnie Clausing from Knellsville, who had astonished everyone by arriving for a recent potluck social alone in the family pick-up. Though women often drove cars, in those days it was practically unheard of for a woman to drive a truck. But, exasperated with waiting for her four brothers to finish shaving and dressing, Minnie had impulsively taken off in the pick-up, leaving them the car.

My mother related the story of this audacious feminist gesture many times to friends and family back home in Chicago, always punctuated with an admiring, "Yep. Imagine that? Drove the pick-up truck herself and in high heels and a dress! Boy, that Minnie, she wasn't waitin' for no goddamn man t' drive her anywhere!"

When gas rationing was instituted following Pearl Harbor, our visits to the farm were curtailed. Later, when peace came and we resumed our visits, life in Port appeared to have continued as before. But the days of the family farm were entering their final decades.

The last time I saw Uncle Pete, he had gone out to the fields before our departure, and I shouted "good-bye" from the back window of my Grandpa Bill's DeSoto as we passed him on the long drive out to the highway. Taking off his hat, he wiped his forehead with a faded red handkerchief, smiled broadly, and waved farewell.

Years later, after I had become a chef, I dreamt one night that I was in the dining room of the old farmhouse. Seated at the table were all the great aunts and uncles that by now had gone: Celia, Polly, Lucille and John, Uncle Pete and Aunt Estelle, Aunt Sophie, my Grandma and her husband Bill. In this wonderful dream I was cooking for them, ham and chickens, mashed potatoes with cream gravy, pickled beets and mixed greens, and of course, Aunt Estelle's legendary kuchen.

Waldorf Salad

Grandma Hazel's mother and father were Flora and Jim MacDonald. Grandma and Grandpa Mac had been married for almost sixty years by the time I began visiting them in Sullivan. They had an old sagged-back white horse named Sparkplug that I thought was the most wonderful horse in the world. Knowing I would get to ride old Sparkplug always made the hike over to Grandpa Mac's farm an anticipated adventure.

The last time I saw Grandpa Mac, we had driven over from Grandma Hazel's to say good-bye before leaving to return to Chicago. We found him out by his weathered gray barn, by this time, like the old man leaning against it, beginning its fall into ruin.

"Granddad," Jimmy greeted him, "how are you?"

Grandpa Mac pushed himself away from the ramshackle building. "Oh, I guess just about no account, I reckon," he answered, struggling toward us on his arthritic knees. "Like this old barn."

The following August, at the age of ninety-three, he passed away.

Grandpa Mac was laid out in the front parlor of their daughter Cleo's house on the other side of the fields from the farm. I accompanied Jimmy to the funeral. We slept upstairs at Cleo's, and the thought of spending the night in the same house with Grandpa Mac's dead body was unnerving. I kept waking up, thinking that I had seen him, standing at the foot of my bed, like a sinister image out of a story from the *Tales Of The Crypt* comic book.

The morning he was to be buried, he was taken to the little funeral home in Sullivan. The entire town turned out for the service. The ladies cooled themselves with the help of the complimentary cardboard fans that had a drawing of the funeral home with a line quoted from the 23rd Psalm on one side and, on the back, photos and advertisements for tombstones.

In a black dress, her dark-rimmed glasses steamed with the heat and tears, Grandma Mac sat in the front row on a sofa, her son Virgil and his wife Goldie on either side of her, her other children surrounding them on couches and easy chairs.

Everyone drove out to the cemetery in a funeral procession of old pick-up trucks and pre-war cars and we assembled around the grave, farmers in dark suits and white shirts with wide ties and good shoes, their wives somber in navy or dark brown, shaking their heads in disbelief.

Grandpa and Grandma MacDonald had been married for sixty-three years. The preacher spoke of Jim and Flora's great accomplishment of living and loving and caring for other people those sixty-three years, and, of a gratified God Who had called His boy home.

The casket was lowered into the ground. The family each dropped a handful of dirt onto the box in a ritual gesture of good-bye. Flowers were taken from the great pile to be pressed in family Bibles for mementos. Then, as with the end of all our lives, those who had endured turned and walked away into the remainder of their own.

When the family returned to the house, followed by friends and neighbors, they found the tables had been laid out, filled with food that the Ladies' Auxiliary from their church had brought. A roasted turkey, a meat loaf, a baked ham, two potato salads; two lime Jell-O molds, one layered with pineapple, the other filled with cucumbers; plates of cold cuts and breads. The highlight was Alma Cutsinger's Waldorf salad. Instead of regular mayonnaise, she had mixed the whipped cream into Miracle Whip instead, and added a bag of those little colored marshmallows. People talked about it for weeks.

Aunt Cleo and Grandma Hazel stayed at the

house with Grandma Mac the next few days, and shortly afterward the venerable old lady, well into her eighties, was moved into Cleo's first floor bedroom, across from the bathroom, near the front porch where she could sit and look back across the cornfield to the farm.

Most of her furniture went to her ten children, grandchildren, and great-grandchildren, but a few pieces had come with her to Cleo's house: the bed and dresser she and Jim had bought as newlyweds, Jim's favorite chair, some photos and crocheted doilies, handmade coverlets and quilts. Her life shrunk down to the contents of a single room.

The farmhouse she and Jim had built with their own hands sat vacant. From time to time Cleo would drive her mother over, and together they'd walk through the house with a dust rag and mop, wiping up water from any leaks, checking to make certain all the windows were locked.

Unable to sell the farm, the family finally decided to raze the house to save on the taxes. And with stoic acceptance of the practicality of the plan, Grandma Mac agreed.

On the weekend of the demolition, Virgil and Goldie came and drove her back to Terre Haute with them where she stayed through to Sunday. They went to church and had Sunday dinner together, arriving back in Sullivan long after dark.

The next morning, Grandma Mac got up early and made a pot of coffee. With the sun coming up, she walked out onto the front porch and looked across the field.

All of it was gone. The house and out-buildings, the old barn, the homestead that had seen their children born and grow and leave, be married and in time bring their children and even their children's children, had disappeared. That wonderful kitchen where, for more than sixty years, her family had sat at tables of fried chicken and mashed potatoes, pot roasts, and hams, strawberry pies, bowls of green beans, plates of biscuits and hand-churned butter, Christmas candy and five generations of Easter eggs. Now a memory.

On our yearly vacation that following summer, we were invited to Cleo and Doc's for breakfast one morning. I was sent to tell Grandma Mac that we were sitting down. I went to her bedroom door and was about to say hello but stopped.

Her back turned to me, she stood alone, one hand resting on a red cabbage rose in the flowered wallpaper, the other covering her eyes, weeping softly.

That fall she herself was laid to rest next to Jim.

Now, more than half a century later, I look at my brother's grandchildren, the great-, great-, great-grandchildren of Grandma Mac, and I can see a trace of her smile in their smiles, the same distant look she had when she told me about her past, as they have dreaming about their future. And here, in the middle of this scope of time between those far and away generations, it is a great comfort—and pleasure—to know I have held hands with them both.

Cannoli-Filled Wedding Cake

ᘉ

B y the mid-forties we had moved into a converted storefront on Osage Avenue at Chicago's far west side. At the age of ten I was not embarrassed that this flat of two rooms had previously been the corner grocery store. To me it was just a place to live. But for my mother it was a mortification.

One morning she undertook the project of scraping the trim around the front windows in preparation for painting, using a kitchen chair for a ladder.

One of the women from the neighborhood appeared wearing a faded housedress under an open coat with bedroom slippers over her husband's socks, a little girl in tow.

"Hey missus!" she called. "Vhat kinds beezness you gonna open dere?"

My mother turned, scraper in hand, "What do

you mean business?" she asked looking down from the elevation of the chair, her voice tense with suppressed annoyance. "I'm living here!"

"Ohhh," said the woman, clearly surprised. "Ha, I 'tought wid dem kinds veendows you gonna open store."

"Dem kinds veendows happen to be picture windows," Milly informed her, mimicking back the woman's accent, adding a "dupa yosh" under her breath.

Our neighborhood was a characteristic blend of nationalities, one of those post World War I communities from which people took that first step out of the "old neighborhood" and into something a little better, on the outskirts of the city, but not yet suburbia.

Shortly after we moved in, I became enamored of Louisa Persino, the little Italian girl who lived a few doors down from our house. There were nine children in Louisa's family: six brothers and three sisters. People used to say the reason Italians had so many children was from all the tomato sauce they ate. An idea which may have had its origins in the Italian translation for tomato, pomme d'amore, "the apple of love."

One afternoon, Louisa gave me a flaky half-eaten cream-filled dessert.

"What's that?" I asked.

"Cannoli," she replied, amazed by my ignorance. "You never ate cannoli?"

Cautiously, I nibbled the end of the crusty shell, tasting a little of the filling. The sweet, creamy rich taste of the ricotta and the crisp, light crunch of the shell enthralled me. My grandmother's tapioca and Jell-O butterscotch pudding, the kind you bought in little boxes and cooked with milk, slipped into second place on my list of creamy desserts as I devoured the last of the confection.

That spring, Louisa's family announced the engagement of their son and brother Clarence to his girlfriend, Mary. In the 1940s facial hair was considered old fashioned, but Clarence had a full moustache, as dark as his slicked back hair and he seemed to me the embodiment of every daydream I'd ever had about Europe and its antique glamour.

And, when I heard Nat King Cole sing "Mona Lisa," I thought he must have certainly been singing about Mary smiling, her dark hair worn loose about her shoulders, her eyes the color of bittersweet chocolate.

Louisa and I adored them.

I think of this handsome couple sitting on the front steps of the Persino's shingled bungalow. Mary on the step beneath Clarence, his arms around her, leaning in so close they might have melted into one body, murmuring softly to one another so that you could just barely see the movement of their lips. In perfect self-sufficiency, the world shut out to their intimacy, I regarded them with an ambivalent mixture of envy and ardor.

They were the two most beautiful people I had ever seen.

On one of those uncommon Chicago days, late in the summer when the humidity was low and the sky a dark blue, Mary and Clarence were married at St. Calista. I watched from our front steps as Louisa's family left for the church, Clarence handsomely resplendent in his white dinner jacket tuxedo. Louisa waved as she stepped into the family car, which they had decorated with streamers and white crepe paper flowers.

I never got to see Mary in her white dress, but Louisa saved me a piece of the wedding cake. Wrapped in a white paper napkin trimmed in silver, the corners brought up and twisted to preserve the fragility of its contents: three layers of golden sponge cake, lightly brushed with rum, and replete with a cannoli-filling of sweetened ricotta, pistachios, cherries, and bits of dark chocolate, all perfectly iced and decorated with an Italian butter cream.

When I think back on that memorable cake, I can see Clarence and Mary on the front steps of the family house, still young, still beautiful, and still caught in the dream of love.

Cooking Directions

⌒

On Saturday nights we ate hot dogs and beans, fried chicken on Sundays, and for the rest of the week a variety of standard mid-west dishes: hamburgers, meat loaf, sloppy Joe's, Salisbury steak, creamed chip beef on toast, salmon patties from canned salmon and on Fridays either frozen halibut cut from a huge piece with a hack saw, or my mother's tuna casserole—one can of tuna, a can of Campbell's Cream of Mushroom Soup, one can of evaporated milk, and a can of peas all layered with wide noodles then topped off with crunched up potato chips, and baked until it became unyielding.

But as far as I was concerned, nothing could top that incomparable 1950s lunchtime repast: a toasted Velveeta Cheese sandwich with a bowl of Campbell's Tomato Soup and a bottle of Pepsi Cola.

Soon after we moved into the storefront on Osage Avenue, my mother went back to waitressing, and I undertook the responsibility of watching over my brother and setting out the supper that she would have begun to prepare before leaving. I was expected to have it ready when Jimmy returned from work at five-thirty. Eventually I took over the entire preparation of these meals.

To save myself from the tedium of this chore, I began to experiment with ingredients and cooking techniques. As an eleven-year-old devotee of Hollywood, movie food was my inspiration.

In the elegant dining rooms and restaurants of the beautiful and well to do, whose stories I watched unfolding on the silver screen, I saw larger than life people dining on (larger than life) flaming "crepes Suzette," "baked Alaska," "filet mignon," "petit fours," "canapés," and "paté de fois gras." I saw food skewered and set ablaze, sculptures carved from ice holding tiny bowls of caviar, and pheasant breasts arriving at the table under a glass bell.

But the most exotic sounding food to me was frogs' legs. I aspired to one day have enough money to be able to take Louisa out to dine at a "ritzy" restaurant where I fantasized myself dressed in a tuxedo, sitting at a table covered with fine white linen, Louisa in a "formal" with an orchid corsage on her wrist (so it wouldn't be crushed while we were dancing).

"The lady will have the filet mignon, rare, and

I'll have the frogs' legs," I would instruct the head-waiter, ordering for us both as the gentleman always did.

Now, in the movies, anytime an actor ordered filet mignon, a t-bone or a strip steak, it was always "blood rare." But none of these scripts had taken the occasion to inform me that not all meat should be served in this manner. Some meat needed to be well done, particularly the cheaper cuts that working families, like my own, usually ate.

My father was horrified by the blood red center of a pork roast I served one evening and insisted it be returned to the oven and cooked for another two hours (trichinosis from insufficiently cooked pork being a real threat in those days).

Another evening he asked suspiciously, "What happened to the string beans?"

I admitted that I had seasoned them with pumpkin pie spices.

"Well what the hell did you do that for?" he demanded.

"I wanted to see what they would taste like."

"Crap," he told me. "They taste like crap."

But, despite these discouragements, I continued, undaunted, with my experimentation. For example; adding different flavors of Kool-Ade to Ann Page angel food cake mixes—grape and lime Kool-Ade were my favorites. One night for dessert I made a lime angel food cake and poured Hershey's chocolate syrup over it.

"For chrissakes," my father complained, "can't you just leave things alone?"

But I could not. I mixed canned vegetables into scrambled eggs in an effort to make an omelet, which I had only seen on a movie screen—I once splashed a little Benedictine Brandy on fried eggs after I heard Betty Grable order eggs benedict between dance numbers.

By the time I was thirteen, I was able to take anything we had in the house and make it taste good. I would fry Brussels sprouts the way I had seen my grandma do, cutting off the stems, slicing them in halves, and frying them in butter until they were, as she called it, "scotched"—today they say "caramelized." I began using sour cream in the mashed potatoes, and making a breading for pork chops using a mix of leftover bread and oatmeal, or fixing stuffed cabbage with barley instead of rice, and everyone anticipated my pumpkin pies that I made with four eggs, heavy cream, and maple syrup (actually dark Karo syrup with a little imitation maple thrown in).

Although my mother employed my cooking for our daily meals, and family and friends relished the meals I prepared, it never occurred to any of us—myself included—that cooking could earn me a living.

When I was growing up, most people regarded cooking as a girl's interest. That a boy should cook was amusing at best; at worst, suspicious.

Once, after I had made a rice pudding and colored it pink with maraschino cherry juice, my grandmother suggested with raised eyebrow, "Milly, maybe there's something wrong with him."

Yet food was becoming an engrossing concern to me. In the fourth grade Sister Mary Eileen had told us that there were seven basic necessities that sustained life: food, clothing, shelter, heat, light, transportation, and communication. Without all of these, Sister Mary Eileen told us, the human race could not continue. "But" she said, "food was our fuel and the most important. It makes your body and your brain run."

I took to heart Sister Mary Eileen's lesson about the prominence of food among the essentials of life. But, at the age of thirteen, it never entered my mind that food and its preparation, skills for which I had such an affinity, could be a career path.

Milly's ambition was, for me, to become a professional: a doctor, a lawyer, or at least an insurance salesman. But I had begun to harbor a grander scheme. The melodrama and glamour of the movies and the emerging television comedies and variety shows that were becoming increasingly a part of our lives had nurtured in me a youthful desire to escape the fate of a two-room storefront. One day I would go to New York City and, as a writer/actor/dancer, and singer, I would become a star.

Pierogi

My mother's brother Arnold and his wife Pauline lived across town from us in a subdivision west of Mannheim Road, not far from the hub cap factory where Uncle Arnold worked the second shift. I was fifteen years old when my Aunt Pauline asked me to babysit my three cousins, Janice, Johnny, and Diann one night while she went out to a baby shower.

I fell asleep on the couch and at daybreak was awakened by the sound of a raucous argument between my aunt and uncle. Suddenly Arnold charged into the living room and belligerently ordered me out of his house.

Although I had done nothing wrong, I feared that there would be further trouble from this incident and that I, was certain somehow, to get the blame. Reluctant to face any inquiry from my mother, I avoided going home. Instead I took a streetcar to the old neighborhood where Uncle Joey, my mother's eldest brother, and his wife Stella, lived in a fourth floor walk-up on Haddon Street with their two daughters, my cousins Judy and Joyce.

I trusted that Stella, with whom I had always felt a rapport, despite my mother's unflattering opinions of her, would understand that I was the injured party.

Aunt Stella hennaed her beautiful hair a Titian red and wore India ink Marlene Dietrich eyebrows that gave her an expression of continual, compassionate, surprise. She kept their little apartment spotless. You couldn't flick a cigarette without her immediately emptying the ashtray and wiping it clean with a damp cloth. She attended Mass every morning and sent my immaculately dressed cousins to Precious Blood, a Polish Catholic school in the neighborhood.

When I arrived that morning, Stella insisted on frying me a bacon sandwich. As I related the story of Arnold's ravings, she shook her head in disbelief. Now, as she set about making some pierogis, we discussed the episode at Aunt Paula and Uncle Arnold's, with all its possible reverberations.

"And what about Paula?" she asked, throwing a handful of flour across the table, and rolling out the ball of dough flat and thin.

I told her that I had heard Paula threatening Arnold that she was "going back to Texas and taking the kids."

"Oh Jesus," my aunt sighed, shaking her head.

"My God, those poor children. Arnold is crazy. Always crazy. I knew that he was crazy when he stood up for your Uncle Joe at our wedding."

Mixing farmers cheese into mashed potatoes, she went on, explaining, "He didn't think it was right that your mother should be a bridesmaid because she was already showing. Joey and Floyd were mad too, but nothing like Arnold."

"Can't women be bridesmaids when they're gonna have babies?" I asked.

"Oh sure," She replied. "But you know, your mother wasn't married."

I put the bacon sandwich down.

"She wasn't?" I asked.

"Well, no, Buddy. That's why Arnold was having such a fit."

Cutting circles out of the dough with a water glass, she began to place spoonfuls of the potato cheese mixture into each of the rounds, folded them over, and sealed the edges with a wet fork.

"You mean she wasn't married to my father when she had me?" I asked.

Looking up from her work she answered uneasily, "Well, Jimmy's not your real father but you knew that, didn't you?"

I hadn't known. Stella's indiscretion had broken a tacit silence that prevailed in the family regarding my illegitimate birth. Under cover of this open secret,

Milly had allowed the supposition to be made that I was Jimmy's offspring. As I took it all in, I suddenly understood why I was told my birth certificate had been lost.

I remembered Milly posing for a photo up in Port wearing Evelyn's wedding dress. She and Jimmy had eloped, she explained, and never had a church wedding or pictures taken in a white dress. Sadly, when the photo was developed, a large hen could be seen walking across the lawn close behind her.

At that time, unwed motherhood was still considered a great disgrace. It marked the child as the offspring of licentiousness.

"Do you know who my real father was?" I asked hopefully.

Stella told me she had never met him, and having revealed too much already, she was anxious to avoid any further inquiries concerning my parentage.

"Take some pierogi home to your mother," she suggested, busying herself with wrapping several of the pierogi in waxed paper, which she put into a brown paper bag left over from the A&P.

I felt it was time for me to go.

On the Milwaukee Avenue streetcar home, I thought about what Stella had told me. I considered the mystery of my real father's identity. Where did he live? Did I look like him? Would we like each other? Would he be rich and buy me a car?

And it suddenly occurred to me that all those people that I had known and loved in Indiana were not really my family anymore.

Transferring onto the Belmont Avenue bus I thought about Jimmy and Milly and my brother Jerry as though they were the "family" and I was an outsider. I felt detached.

Stella's revelation had permanently altered my relations with my mother and, not long afterward, I left to go to school one morning and never returned.

Red Sauce

⌒℧⌒

By the time I was eighteen I had moved in with Joe, a thirty-four-year-old Italian plumber who lived on 115th Street in Roseland, an Italian neighborhood on the far south side.

Joe and I lived in the back of his heating and refrigeration shop. Living in the back of a store was, I thought, a step up from the store-front.

Joe's business partner, Rudy, lived upstairs from us in the back apartment with his wife Ethel and their son Pookie. Joe's third wife Nukki, from whom he was currently separated, lived in the upstairs front apartment with their two children, Linda and Joey, who were then six and two.

After Ethel got pregnant with their second child, she and Rudy bought a house a few blocks from the shop, and Harriette, one of Ethel's three sisters, moved into their vacated apartment.

Within weeks, a third sister, Dorothy, who was

actually Joe's second wife, moved up from Florida to live with Harriette. I should also tell you that Joe's first wife, Lorraine, lived only blocks away, and sometimes I would join the three of them for coffee, and we would discuss his failings.

Joe was one of the handiest men I have ever met. He could fix any motor and was adept at all those repairs that are necessary to keep an apartment or a house running. A culinary mentor to me, he made a red sauce better than any I had ever tasted.

My mother's recipe for a red sauce was one small can of tomato sauce, one can of Campbell's tomato soup, a pound of round steak ground twice, an onion, and one cup of water—all cooked together in the pressure cooker to produce a rust-colored sauce that she served on well-cooked Red Cross spaghetti, and sprinkled generously with Kraft's grated American cheese.

It was my favorite dish.

But Joe's red sauce was a "culinary revelation."

"First heat the olive oil until it smokes. Then add the meat," he said, placing the inexpensive cuts of roast into the cast iron pot. "Y'gotta brown the meat in the oil with a few bay leaves," he explained. "Brown it on all sides."

When this was done, he removed the meat to a platter, set it aside, and opening a can of tomato paste that he added to the pot, he turned the heat to a medium low flame.

"You should brown the tomato paste in the meat drippings, slow like, keep stirring it so it don't burn and always remember," he said, tapping my forehead with his index finger to emphasize the principle, "The darker brown you can get your tomato paste, the better your sauce'll taste. That's the secret."

When the tomato paste had sufficiently browned, Joe added a large can of plum tomatoes, two large cans of tomato sauce, a couple of chopped onions and green peppers, a bulb of fresh garlic, chopped fine, a handful each of dried basil and rosemary, a pound of mushrooms, a couple of cups of water and half a bottle of Chianti. Returning the meat to the pot, he'd let it cook on a low flame all day long, from eight in the morning to six at night, until the meat fell from the bones. After it was cooled, he stored it overnight in the ice box (refrigerator). It was not until dinner the next day that it would it be served over a pasta, sprinkled with freshly grated Romano Pecorino, and eaten with loaves of hard-crusted bread fresh from the Italian bakery across the alley.

Joe and I remained friends for the rest of his long life. At eighty, he suffered a heart attack and spent a month recuperating at a hospital on the north side.

At the same time, his son Joey became grandfather to a baby boy born with a pre-cancerous condition, who had been sent to Chicago for treatment. Living eighty-five miles away in Indiana, the baby's mother was unable to afford the time away from work to travel to see the child, who, by sheer coincidence, was being cared for at the same hospital where Joe was recovering. And so, for the next month, it was Joe who held this baby, his great-grandson, every day until they were both declared well enough to leave.

That winter Jack and I spent Christmas at Joe's. One evening he threw a dinner party in our honor, a memorable meal of roast chicken with garlic, lemon, and rosemary, and his—for me—inspiring red sauce served over his mostaccioli.

Seated around the table with Joe were Jack and myself, Joe's ex-wife Nookie with Rudy (who she had married after Ethel died), Joe's son Joey and his wife, Joe's daughter and her girlfriend.

Another perspective on family values.

Life Upon the Wicked Stage

༄

While I was living with Joe, I became involved with Chicago's Encore Theatre, a semi-professional theatre company on Clark Street at the heart of Skid Row. It was at Encore that I met Ellen Albrecht, a statuesque redhead with a knockout voice who, after consulting a numerologist, changed her name from Ellen Albrecht to "Ellie Brite."

In the fall of 1960, with "Moon River" playing on the radio of her 1949 Chevy, Ellie and I embarked for the Big Apple to pursue stardom. Seventeen non-stop hours later, we arrived in New York, where I called our old friend Tony, another associate from Encore. Tony, who had left Chicago for New York, had opened a beauty shop in Astoria.

He was ecstatic to hear from us, and we were overjoyed when he told us that he knew of an apartment where we could crash for the time being, although our occupancy was to be circumscribed by certain odd restrictions.

First, we must never use the telephones, of which there were an unusual number in those pre-cellular days.

And secondly, the premises must be vacated each day between the hours of eleven and two, when, as Tony explained, it was being used as a trysting-place for adulterous lovers.

Unwilling to look this gift horse in the mouth, we accepted these stipulations without hesitation, but they became the subject of our bemused speculations. Who were these lovers, and why was it so important that we not use the phone, since there were five of them?

Some weeks later, Ellie, and I decided to move from Astoria to Manhattan. On the day we were to vacate the apartment, we were running late and were just picking up our bags at eleven o'clock, when the door opened and a woman entered, accompanied by two gentlemen. We apologized profusely for our tardiness but they seemed unconcerned and were quite friendly. Leaving our keys on the table as had been arranged, we wished them good-bye and hustled out, exchanging amused looks once the door was closed behind us.

So these were the lovers?

Speculating on the *ménage à trois* we now supposed had been going on, we reached the street and were discussing the possibility of hiring a taxi, when suddenly four police cars pulled up outside and several men ran up the stairs and into the building. We watched from the other side of the street to see what would happen and were flabbergasted when the officers emerged a short time later with the three-way in handcuffs.

Tony later confessed that the lovers tryst had been a fabrication and that the apartment had actually been used by three bookies for taking bets on the races. That's why there were five phones. Had we been another two minutes leaving the apartment, we would have gone to jail with the three of them.

My dream in coming to New York was to pursue a career in writing and show business. Noel Coward and Cole Porter were my idols. Their sophisticated lyrics and soigné celebrity style set the standard for my ambition.

I wrote the book and lyrics to a two-act musical I called *The Ladies Of Bank Street*, did summer stock in Connecticut, and even sold a couple of skits for a revue at the Upstairs at The Downstairs. In one of these skits, Lily Tomlin was cast as the girl who had come to New York to become a waitress but could only find jobs as a star.

But of course, selling a few comedy sketches

was not enough to pay the rent. And so, unlike Lily Tomlin's would-be waitress, I was in New York to become a star but could only find work as a waiter.

Cream of Watercress Soup

I took a job at an upscale restaurant in the East Forties called Pablo's. Like most of his help, excepting myself and one of the other waiters, Pablo came from South America. His volatile chef was a prickly Argentinean character whose outbursts could be intimidating.

One evening, the other North American waiter had the misfortune to let a plate of duck in a red cherry sauce slide off his tray and onto the floor. The chef actually threatened to punch him. Berating him violently in Spanish, he ran the duck under the faucet to wash it off, threw it back on the grill for a couple of minutes, plated and re-sauced it, then returned it to the waiter vowing in what English he possessed, that if the duck went on the floor again, the waiter would too.

In spite of such scenes, I succeeded in becoming somewhat friendly with this temperamental character when, one evening, intrigued by a pot of cream soup peppered with beautiful green flecks floating on the top, I asked, "What is this?"

"Cream of Watercress," he answered begrudgingly.

Refusing to be intimidated by his surly response, I asked if I could taste it and he conceded, giving me the fish eye, but pleased in spite of himself. Light and creamy, with the delicious fresh essence of watercress, barely salted and peppered, it was the most incredible soup I had ever eaten and I told him so. From then on he was happy to answer any culinary questions I had. And though I could not speak Spanish and he barely knew English, I learned a great deal from this accomplished chef, simply by watching him as he prepared food.

He made cannelloni using a crepe instead of pasta, filled with ground meat, spinach, and thinly sliced turkey breast, baked in a little casserole of red sauce and topped with a brandied cream laced with Gruyère cheese.

He did the aforementioned duck in a sour cherry and mustard sauce sweetened with brown sugar and Kirsch that was outstanding. And it was in his kitchen that I first tasted paella.

Like my grandmother, he never consulted a recipe. Like my grandmother, he always cooked straight from the hand out of his innate knowledge. His talent for cooking gave him an inspiring freedom in the kitchen.

Peanut Butter Sauce

∽

My final job as a waiter in New York City was at a West Village restaurant called "Chumley's."

In keeping with its origin as a speakeasy in the twenties, Chumleys had no sign. You entered off Bedford Street through a painted door marked only with the street number "86." The expression "to 86 someone," is purportedly derived from the police warnings to imbibers before Prohibition raids. "Hey 86! Get your crowd out the back door! Here come the cops!"

Inside the door, a few steps ascended to a landing where you turned, then descended a few steps down into a dark, arts-and-crafts dining room, with hammered metal lighting fixtures, oak paneling, and framed book-jackets of its famous patrons. Writers like Willa Cather and John Dos Passos—poets, journalists, and activists from the Lost Generation to the Beat Generations.

The rectangular bare wood eating tables were scarred with decades of patrons' initials. There was a fireplace where a fire was kept burning during the winter months, and stained glass windows behind the bar, illuminating the shelves of spirits.

As I heard the story, a Mr. Lee and a Mr. Chum bought the property after passage of the 21st Amendment, repealing the ban on alcohol, and opened a Chinese restaurant. After Mr. Chum died, his widow bought out Mr. Lee and switched from serving Chinese to American fare, reopening the restaurant as Chumley's.

When I worked at Chumley's, it had become an after-hours hangout for theatrical people. I waited on Irene Pappas many nights when she was performing *Iphigenia at Aulis*. She would often come in after the shows and order a hamburger. I remember one evening being dazzled by the grace with which she undid her hair. It was the same gesture I had admired in her performance as the beautiful widow in *Zorba The Greek*, as she is about to make love to Alan Bates. The room lit up.

The *Out of Towners*, with Jack Lemmon, shot locations at Chumley's, and the cast of *Jacques Brel Is Alive And Well And Living In Paris* would come in every night after the show to eat and sing, leaving wonderful tips and free tickets to see them at the Village Gate.

The cook at that time was an Indonesian gentleman named Soo Yoo, the most collected chef I have ever known. I only saw him lose his cool once and, in so doing, tossed a plate across the kitchen so gently it didn't even break.

Soo Yoo's specialty was a dish he called Indonesian rice: hunks of beef tenderloin over rice and vegetables with a peanut butter sauce and a fried egg on top. Before this, having only known peanut butter as something spread on a slice of bread with jelly, I loved it. In 1967 it was a lesson in fearless combinations that I never forgot.

Tasting the food in the restaurants where I worked and sampling the different cuisines that could be found in Manhattan inspired my natural inclination to experiment with cooking. I took to heart Soo Yoo's lesson of fearless combinations and Mrs. Bronstein's dictum to "always add a little extra."

A friend of mine who was working public relations for an importer of Spanish sherry gave me a case of mixed brands, and since I didn't drink much, I began using it for cooking. Duff Gordon in a cream sauce on chicken breasts stuffed with asparagus, Sandeman in a sour cream sauce on Cornish hens with mushrooms, and Harveys Bristol Cream in apple pies and chocolate pudding.

My friends thought these dinners were wonderful. Whenever we were down to our last few bucks we'd buy a quart of strawberries, a pint of sour cream, and a pound of brown sugar, dipping the strawberries into the sour cream, then the brown sugar.

One day an acquaintance who played Fender guitar for a small band that often ate at Chumley's invited me to meet his guru, a charismatic Dutch woman in her mid-sixties who held weekly philosophical discussions in her living room. She told me that I was afraid of success, and hung a small, oval piece of Lapis Lazuli around my neck, which, she said, had the power to dispel the fear of good things happening to me. It was 1969. The new age magical attitude that "all things were possible if you just believed it" was taking hold of my life. I grew my hair long, added a moustache and a beard, and prepared myself for a life of success.

Ceres Street

⌒⌒

As I was pursuing my theatrical ambitions, an alternative occupation, of which I was completely unaware, was beginning to unfold through of a series of seemingly unrelated occurrences.

First, a phone call from Gene Brown, an old friend from Chicago.

Gene had taken a position in New Hampshire as director of a children's theater program, and he invited me for a visit. He was renting a place in Dover called Tiny House. Built on plans for a carriage house in Williamsburg, Tiny House looked out over fields and tidal marshes to the Bellamy River where it enters Little Bay.

It had a baronial fireplace of local fieldstone; a loft bedroom, an adequate kitchen, and a comfortable guest bedroom where I slept during my frequent visits. "Frequent" because in those days you could fly from La Guardia to Logan between eleven in the morning and two in the afternoon for eleven dollars.

New York was stimulating. I was making a good living with a relatively short workweek and I had a circle of great friends. But the city was also a distraction. I had not finished an extended piece of writing for too many months.

I have always had a belief that your destiny presents you with previews of what's to come and when Gene told me about a vacant schoolhouse that was being rented for only twenty-five dollars a month in South Berwick, Maine, I suddenly recalled studying one of the ads on a Chicago bus going someplace when I was a kid. The ad read: "From Maine to California, more people choose Alka Seltzer."

On one side of the ad a shapely young women in sunglasses and a bathing suit, lounged under an umbrella on the shores of the Pacific. On the other side was a rosy cheeked boy in a scarf and wool cap, rugged hills behind him with pine trees covered in snow. Somehow I had known at that moment that I would live in Maine. And now, decades later, I was moving there.

I took a leave from Chumley's for the summer, sublet my East 90th Street apartment to Charles Shultz's maid, and headed for Maine to write my first novel. I think of what the money was in the late sixties. My apartment rent was ninety dollars a month. I had sublet it for two hundred a month, and the rent in the schoolhouse was twenty-five dollars a month. With everything paid, it left me eighty-five dollars a month to live.

The schoolhouse was rustic but well appointed. It had a fireplace and a sink with running hot water. There was a cook stove and a woodstove, and an outhouse surrounded by lilacs. I skinny-dipped in the Great Works River down the hill when I needed a bath and slept in the attic on an old horsehair mattress.

When I wasn't writing I spent many afternoons at nearby Ogunquit beach. It was there, one day in early August, that I met Mark, who was to become a future business partner. When passing me on the beach he stopped, pointed to the guru's piece of lapis and asked, "Excuse me, but why do you wear a blue strawberry around your neck?"

This overture led to our friendship, and when the summer ended, Mark returned to Manhattan with me.

That winter I had the good fortune of selling one of my skits to a comedy team and it was performed on several variety shows. After an appearance on *The Merv Griffin Show*, Merv himself praised the skit as a piece of great material. On being told that I was in the audience he invited me to stand up for an applause. It was a moment of triumph, and immediately following the show, I was signed by an agent for William Morris who was also in the audience, with the promise that I would soon be writing for television.

That spring, the owner of my apartment building offered me fifteen hundred dollars to buy out my lease and Mark and I accepted this windfall as an opportunity to return to the schoolhouse in Maine.

It was a beautiful summer. We planted a huge garden in bucolic retreat, and spent long afternoons at the beach while awaiting my first writing assignment.

And then, one afternoon in September, I went to get the mail and found a Manila envelope containing all the material I had submitted to the agency months before. It had all been rejected.

I was thirty-three years old, I had no money, no job, and no idea what the future would bring or even what to look for. My dream of stardom had evaporated. At a complete loss, I leaned against the mailbox and, looking heavenward, announced dramatically, "I'm at the end of my rope!" In response to this declaration, there followed the best advice I've ever given to myself. "Well then, let go." Some might call this an epiphany. I think it was just insight.

It is human nature to look upon the things that happen to us as either "good fortune" or "bad luck," but each offers a new beginning. When I review the map of my past, I now begin to recognize how events were weaving together, directing me to where I was supposed to go.

Through what proved to be a fortuitous coincidence of misfortunes, a few days later, Gene too, found himself without a job when the funding for the children's theater project was abruptly canceled.

That evening he had dinner with us. We ate a baked ham in raspberries and Grand Marnier with curried mashed sweet potatoes and carrots. As we commiserated over our situation I was thinking I could wait tables again, although with the fall approaching and the summer restaurants closing for the season, the timing was inauspicious. Gene could always find a job teaching, but it was too late for him to land anything other than a substitute position. Neither of us was very enthused about these prospects.

It was then that Mark jokingly suggested, "Why don't we open a restaurant? At least we'll always eat."

"As long as I can be the cook." I added off handedly.

We continued to consider other venues of survival, but throughout the evening, we kept returning with growing interest to Mark's idea. What had begun as a quip was gradually contemplated as a possibility, and before we parted that evening, the suggestion of opening our own restaurant had emerged as a direction out of our present difficulties.

First, we drew up a list of everything we thought that we would need. Even before we found our location, we began perusing the numerous second hand shops in and around Portsmouth. I purchased two archaic apartment-sized stoves for fifteen dollars apiece and two twenty-year-old refrigerators for another thirty dollars. My entire collection of pots, pans, and kettles was purchased second hand for under ten dollars.

We bought forty unmatched pressed wood dining room chairs at two or three dollars each; dinner plates, cake plates, and dessert plates at a quarter each; and bread-and-butter-sized dishes for a dime. We purchased white dime store mugs for soup and coffee and splurged on twenty new tables so that they would all be the same size. A friend who was a salesman for Wedgewood donated his forty sample plates which we used as under-liners.

Tiny House became tiny storage.

In New York I had frequented a place called Casa Brazil, where dinner was served in two seatings, one at seven, one at nine. That seemed like a sensible way to run a restaurant. No line cooking, no missed order stubs, no one screaming for their order. It meant nothing more than cooking a wonderful dinner for forty people twice a night. Somehow I knew I could easily do that.

We searched through the neighborhoods of Portsmouth, considering the various defunct eateries currently for sale or rent. But nothing met our expectations. We didn't want a restaurant, we wanted a dining room. And as people began to hear about our plan of "two seatings an evening" the replies and advice from real estate agents were generous, but not supportive.

"Oh, that'll never work," was the most frequent comment. There were others: "Nobody wants to be told when they have to come to dinner." And the most offered, "you can't just offer three entrees and give everybody the same thing."

And to all of these pronouncements the three of us simply thought, "well, why not?"

And then, on November 1, 1970, coming down Bow Street, we made a right turn onto the narrow cobbled street that runs next to the river where the tugboats docked. Ceres Street.

As we drove slowly along, we saw a renovation was underway on one of the nineteenth-century warehouses. Looking in through the windows, we discovered a long hall-like room with brick walls, a beamed ceiling, a back wall of polished granite boulders, and a fireplace with an impressive rough-hewn mantel. This was everything we could hope for, and we went inside to make inquiries.

The foreman, who was also the owner of the building, was intrigued by our idea, and the next day, November 2nd, called to offer us a lease to Number 29 Ceres Street. When he told us he had already begun to put up wall board and cover the beams in the ceiling we told him to take them down, that the wonderful thing about the space was the old brick walls and beamed ceilings. He agreed.

"What are you going to call it?" he asked.

The question at this point was still unresolved.

"How about Blue Strawbery?" Mark suggested.

On November 18th, 1970, sixteen days after signing the lease, at the remarkable cost of twenty-seven hundred dollars in total, we opened to a full house.

I began the meal with a hot watercress vichyssoise, followed by mushrooms in a red sauce stuffed with escargot. As I was putting together a dressing for the salad, I realized I was out of olive oil. In that moment of panic I thought, what the heck do I do now? And then, out of the blue, it came to me.

I quickly threw some fresh cranberries, a splash of maple syrup, some Dijon mustard, the juice of a lemon and a couple handfuls of ice into the blender to create, what may have been the world's first, frosted salad dressing.

For the entree, I served a tenderloin of beef in a white wine peanut butter sauce with mushrooms. Everyone was offered carrots baked in curry and honey; potatoes roasted in sour cream, zucchini in dill and butter, and string beans fried in bacon.

For dessert, we heaped fresh strawberries onto a platter with brown sugar and sour cream, just as we had back in New York when we were down to our last dollar. It became our hallmark dessert.

Dinner began promptly at eight that first night, and ended at one fifteen in the morning to a round of applause. That night, cooking for all those people for the first time in my life somehow gave me the most complete sense of freedom I had ever known.

The next afternoon the local paper gave us a glowing review, praising the food at Blue Strawbery and referring to me as "Chef Haller."

Chef! Suddenly, out of nowhere, and to my complete surprise, I had become a chef.

They don't always come packaged as we think they should, or even expect, but without a doubt, our dreams do come true.

Epilogue

❦

Osage Avenue and Louisa

Almost twenty years ago the *Olde Farmer's Almanac* printed an essay of mine entitled "My Golden Anniversary with Pizza," in which I had related the story of my first experience tasting pizza in the summer of 1947 in Mrs. Persino's kitchen. I was ten years old, and Mrs. Persino was my girlfriend Louisa's mother. Although Louisa and I had not spoken since our adolescence some fifty years before, I had never forgotten her. From the ages of ten to fifteen she had been my closest friend, my primary confidante, an ally in my struggles and aspirations. Louisa was the girl I assumed I would one day marry.

A year after the essay had been printed I received a letter from Kate Persino who lived in Wisconsin. She was married to Jimmy, one of Louisa's nephews, and while going through some out-of-date magazines she had come across the *Almanac*. Leafing through it, the piece on pizza caught her eye and she was startled to discover the name "Persino" with a story of her grandmother-in-law's kitchen.

Phoning her in-laws, she asked if they recognized the name of the author. But in 1951, after leaving home at the age of fifteen, I had changed my name from Buddy Heien to James Haller.

Searching the Internet with the hope of finding out who I was and where I lived, Kate was surprised to discover another story about the Persino family—the story of the wedding of her husband's uncle Clarence and his wife Mary—"Clarence and Mary's Cannoli Filled Wedding Cake."

Perplexed and even a little anxious, they wondered "How does this guy know so much about our family when we don't know anything about him?"

"We are puzzled," Kate had written. *"No one knows who you are, however you seem to know so much about us. Are you with the CIA?"*

Excited by the possibility of renewing our friendship, I immediately wrote back and explained to her about my name change and that I had lived at the corner of Osage Avenue and School Street in the front of the old store just down the block from the Persino family home.

I enclosed two of my cook books, briefly recounted memories of her grandmother-in-law's kitchen, and expressed a strong wish to hear from Louisa again.

That was in April. The following July, I left for a month's vacation and on my return discovered a letter from Louisa, with the return address only a few blocks from where I had lived a half century before.

Wedging my thumb under the flap of the envelope I drew it along, tearing it open. When I unfolded the pages of her long letter, several scraps of folded paper fell onto the table. I was moved to discover the verses that I had written to Louisa years before. She had preserved them all this time. Reading through them, I could remember as though it were yesterday, sitting on the stoop of the old storefront, and composing them under the light of the gas street lamps.

Her parents and two of her brothers were gone, she wrote, and Mary, the bride whose wedding cake I had always recalled so vividly, had died of cancer at age forty-two.

Louisa had married, though sadly, she was widowed. She and her husband Chuck had raised seven children. The loss of her husband was followed a year later by the loss of her beloved eldest daughter to a rare form of cancer to which she had succumbed only two weeks after the birth of her only child.

"*We did have such a beautiful childhood together,*" the letter continued, "*and I kept you tucked in my heart forever. We bared our souls to each other. It was the sweetest friendship and I did share all those beautiful memories with my children. Love should be talked about with nothing to hide. That's why I'm sending you the notes you wrote me when we were so very young. I kept them all these years because you were a special part of my life."*

Lovingly I gathered up the yellowed scraps of poetry and folded them carefully back into the letter, then called Chicago information for Louisa's number.

So much time had passed since we last had talked, decades, half of a century, our lifetimes.

The phone rang three times before it was answered, "Hello?"—the same voice as when we had last talked.

"Louisa?" I asked.

There was the slightest pause, "Buddy?" she replied.

"Love should be talked about with nothing to hide," Louisa had written.

After this whenever I went back to Chicago we would spend time together. I met her children, who were cordial and welcoming to me. Louisa even came to visit me on two happy occasions. Each time she got off the plane carrying a jar of her home-made red sauce, a cake, and some cookies.

In the time we spent together we cooked and remembered the food her family had made when we were young. It gave a special sweetness to the renewal of this friendship, to share her enjoyment when

I showed her something of the state that I had chosen to make my home. I think we both felt a great happiness in this rekindling. Whatever it was that we had been together, so long ago, we were that again.

Not long after this last visit, she began writing of concerns for her health. She had consulted a heart specialist, who diagnosed her with congenital heart failure. After a collapse that had left her hospitalized for some time, I flew to Chicago to see her. She seemed to be regaining strength before I left to go back to Maine, and her subsequent letters were optimistic and cheerful.

But a few months after my visit, her daughter Mary phoned me from the hospital and asked if I would like to speak to Louisa. With Mary holding the phone to her mother's ear, I quietly whispered how much she had always meant to me, and that I still loved her. It was the last time we spoke. Mary told me afterwards, that she had smiled.

Internationally acclaimed master chef, author, and presenter James Haller has written numerous articles, books, and personal stories about his journey to becoming an award-winning master chef. He was the executive chef, founder, and owner of the Blue Strawbery restaurant in Portsmouth, New Hampshire, and the Lee Fontain Carriage House in Memphis, Tennessee. He also owned and operated James Haller's Kitchen, where he taught classes and acted as a food consultant. Haller is the author of three cookbooks, a food/fitness book, *What to Eat When You Don't Feel Like Eating*, a book for feeding terminally ill people, which has sold over 800,000 copies, as well as *Vie de France*, a book about the month he spent with friends in the Loire Valley for his sixtieth birthday, where he renewed his love of cooking. *Vie de France* has also been published in Brazil and the Czech Republic. Chef Haller received the Granite State Award for Outstanding Public Service in 2000, and The Canadian Robert Pope Wellness Award for *What to Eat When You Don't Feel Like Eating*. Haller spent ten years with Seacoast Hospice as a board member and volunteer, and also taught classes for the Association for the Blind, teaching unsighted people how to cook. Currently he is a frequent guest chef for restaurants in Portsmouth, New Hampshire, including The Wellington Room with Chef Patrice Gerard.

Coming in 2016:

Vie de France

republished as

A Little Kitchen in France

Sharing Food, Friendship, and a
Kitchen in the Loire Valley

"A beguiling tale of a month in France when the living was easy, the friendships warm, and the food superb." — *Kirkus Reviews*

Chef Haller is happy to announce a newly revised edition of this wonderful book under a new title.

When he and his closest friends toasted his sixtieth birthday, he thought that their dream of spending a month together in a beautiful house in Europe would remain just that—a dream. But a year and a half later, Haller and friends arrived at a charming 17th-century chateau in Savonnieres, the small Loire Valley town that would be their home for the next month.

Featuring dozens of delicious recipes, *A Little Kitchen in France* is a delightful testament to the joy of good friends and good food—and a heartfelt exhortation to reach for your wildest, most wonderful dreams.

chefjameshaller.com

Made in the USA
Middletown, DE
10 November 2018